contents

Please note that Australian cup and spoon measurements are metric. A conversion chart appears on page 62.

About mince...

Mince is the main ingredient in many traditional dishes from almost every culture: from rissoles and hamburgers to meatballs and moussaka and beyond, to kibbeh, keema and kofta, the list is endless. No matter how you intend to cook it, raw mince should be purchased just before you head home and stored immediately in the coldest part of your fridge. If you're not going to use it within a few hours, discard its packaging and place it in a non-plastic container covered loosely with foil to allow air to circulate. The longest mince can be kept refrigerated is three days; it can be frozen, wrapped tightly, for up to two months. Mince is graded by the amount of fat it contains; read the label's fine-print to determine the percentage of fat in the package you're considering. Generally, lower fat content is reflected in higher price. Mince with a fat content of 10 per cent or less is considered fairly low in fat; 3 per cent is the optimum low-fat mince. Its fat content also affects the texture of the dish in which it is used: some recipes, such as meatloaf or meatballs, benefit from a slightly higher fat content, while other dishes, such as stir-fries or a bolognese, are better with low-fat mince. When a recipe calls for mince to be cooked "in batches", neither the pan nor the oil should cool between batches, otherwise the mince will stew and flavour will be lost. Too much mince added to a pan crowds it, and reduces the pan's heat, making the mince clump and cook unevenly.

beef rissoles with cabbage mash

2 bacon rashers (140g), rind
    removed, chopped finely
1 small brown onion (80g),
    chopped finely
1 tablespoon
    worcestershire sauce
1 cup (70g) stale
    breadcrumbs
1 egg
¼ cup coarsely chopped
    fresh flat-leaf parsley
500g beef mince
2 tablespoons
    barbecue sauce
1 tablespoon dijon mustard
2 cups (500ml) beef stock
1 tablespoon cornflour
2 tablespoons water
cabbage mash

1kg potatoes, quartered
¼ cup (60ml) cream
30g butter, chopped
200g finely shredded
    savoy cabbage

1 Cook potato for cabbage mash.
2 Cook bacon and onion in medium frying pan, stirring, until onion softens. Remove from heat.
3 Using hand, combine worcestershire sauce, breadcrumbs, egg, parsley, mince and half of the barbecue sauce with bacon mixture in large bowl; shape mixture into eight rissoles.
4 Cook rissoles in same lightly oiled pan, in batches, until browned both sides and cooked through. Cover to keep warm.
5 Place mustard, stock and remaining barbecue sauce in same pan; bring to a boil. Stir in blended cornflour and water; cook, stirring, until gravy boils and thickens slightly.
6 Finish cabbage mash. Serve cabbage mash and rissoles, topped with gravy.
cabbage mash Boil, steam or microwave potato until tender; drain. Mash potato with cream and butter until smooth; stir in cabbage.

serves 4
per serving 24.3g total fat (12.8g saturated fat); 2491kJ (569 cal); 51.2g carbohydrate; 42.8g protein; 1g fibre
tip Rissoles can be prepared a day ahead and kept, covered, in the refrigerator.

chow mein

We used button mushrooms in this recipe, but you can use whichever variety you prefer so long as they are sliced thinly.

1 tablespoon vegetable oil
1 medium brown onion (150g), chopped finely
2 cloves garlic, crushed
500g lean beef mince
1 tablespoon curry powder
1 large carrot (180g), chopped finely
2 trimmed celery stalks (200g), sliced thinly
150g mushrooms, sliced thinly
1 cup (250ml) chicken stock
⅓ cup (80ml) oyster sauce
2 tablespoons soy sauce
450g fresh thin egg noodles
½ cup (60g) frozen peas
½ cup (55g) frozen sliced green beans
½ small chinese cabbage (350g), shredded coarsely

1 Heat oil in wok; stir-fry onion and garlic until onion softens. Add mince; stir-fry until mince is cooked through. Add curry powder; stir-fry about 1 minute or until fragrant. Add carrot, celery and mushrooms; stir-fry until vegetables soften.
2 Add stock, sauces and noodles; stir-fry gently until combined, bring to a boil. Add peas, beans and cabbage, reduce heat; simmer, uncovered, tossing occasionally, 5 minutes or until vegetables are just soft.

serves 4
per serving 14g total fat (4.1g saturated fat); 2483kJ (594 cal); 71.6g carbohydrate; 43.7g protein; 1.3g fibre

pastitsio

250g macaroni

2 eggs, beaten lightly

¾ cup (60g) grated
    parmesan cheese

2 tablespoons stale
    breadcrumbs

meat sauce

1 tablespoons olive oil

2 medium brown onions
    (300g), chopped finely

750g beef mince

400g can chopped tomatoes

⅓ cup (95g) tomato paste

½ cup (125ml) beef stock

¼ cup (60ml) dry white wine

½ teaspoon ground
    cinnamon

1 egg

cheese topping

90g butter

½ cup (75g) plain flour

3½ cups (875ml) milk

1 cup (80g) grated
    parmesan cheese

2 egg yolks

1 Preheat oven to moderate (180°C/160°C fan-forced). Grease shallow 2.5-litre (10-cup) ovenproof dish.

2 Add pasta to large saucepan of boiling water; boil, uncovered, until just tender, drain. Combine warm pasta, egg and cheese in large bowl; mix well. Press pasta over base of dish.

3 Make meat sauce. Make cheese topping.

4 Top pasta evenly with meat sauce, pour over cheese topping; smooth surface then sprinkle with breadcrumbs. Bake, uncovered, about 1 hour or until browned lightly. Stand 10 minutes before serving.

meat sauce Heat oil in large saucepan, add onion; cook, stirring, until onion is soft. Add mince; cook, stirring, until mince changes colour. Stir in undrained tomatoes, tomato paste, stock, wine and cinnamon; simmer, uncovered, until thick. Cool 10 minutes; stir in egg.

cheese topping Melt butter in medium saucepan, add flour, stir over heat until bubbling. Remove from heat, gradually stir in milk. Stir over heat until sauce boils and thickens; stir in cheese. Cool 5 minutes; stir in egg yolks.

serves 6

per serving 41.7g total fat (21.8g saturated fat); 3398kJ (813 cal); 54.4g carbohydrate; 54g protein; 3.8g fibre

tips Can be made a day ahead; keep, covered, in the refrigerator; it is also suitable to freeze. Serve with a salad of leafy greens and tomatoes, if desired.

spaghetti bolognese

This is a quick recipe for bolognese, ensuring it will be on the table in under 40 minutes.

1 tablespoon olive oil
1 medium brown onion (150g), chopped coarsely
2 cloves garlic, crushed
2 medium carrots (240g), chopped coarsely
2 trimmed celery stalks (200g), chopped coarsely
500g beef mince
2 x 400g cans chopped tomatoes
½ cup (125ml) dry red wine
⅓ cup (90g) tomato paste
1 teaspoon white sugar
200g mushrooms, sliced thinly
¼ cup finely chopped fresh basil
375g spaghetti
¼ cup (20g) grated parmesan cheese

1 Heat oil in large saucepan; cook onion, garlic, carrot and celery, stirring, until vegetables soften. Add mince; cook, stirring, until mince is cooked through. Add undrained tomatoes, wine, paste and sugar; cook, stirring, about 15 minutes or until sauce thickens slightly. Add mushrooms and basil, reduce heat; simmer, uncovered, 10 minutes.
2 Meanwhile, cook pasta in large saucepan of boiling water, uncovered, until just tender; drain.
3 Divide pasta among serving bowls; top with bolognese sauce, sprinkle with cheese.

serves 4
per serving 15.8g total fat (5.1g saturated fat); 2874kJ (681 cal); 82.2g carbohydrate; 45.9g protein; 1.5g fibre
tip Serve with ciabatta and a green salad tossed with italian dressing, if desired.

barbecued mini asian-flavoured meatloaves with grilled vegetables

1 tablespoon soy sauce
⅓ cup (80ml) char siu sauce
600g beef mince
4 green onions, sliced thinly
2 cloves garlic, crushed
190g can sliced water
    chestnuts, drained,
    chopped finely
1 fresh small red thai chilli,
    chopped finely
¼ cup (25g) packaged
    breadcrumbs
1 egg
1 large carrot (180g)
300g baby corn cobs
200g baby green beans
1 teaspoon sesame oil
¼ cup (60ml)
    soy sauce, extra

1 Combine soy sauce and char siu sauce in small bowl. Using hand, combine mince, onion, garlic, chestnut, chilli, breadcrumbs, egg and 1 tablespoon of the char siu mixture in large bowl; shape mince mixture into four rectangular meatloaves. Wrap each meatloaf in lightly oiled foil. Cook on heated barbecue flat plate, uncovered, turning occasionally, 15 minutes.

2 Remove foil; brush meatloaves with remaining char siu mixture. Cook on heated oiled flat plate, turning, until browned all over and cooked through.

3 Meanwhile, cut carrot into thick strips. Divide carrot, corn and beans among four lightly oiled 15cm-square pieces of foil, sprinkle with combined oil and extra soy sauce; wrap foil around vegetables.

4 Cook on heated barbecue flat plate, uncovered, about 8 minutes or until vegetables are just tender. Serve sliced meatloaves with vegetables.

serves 4
per serving 14.1g total fat (4.6g saturated fat); 1743kJ (417 cal); 31.6g carbohydrate; 40.8g protein; 2.3g fibre
tip Sprinkle meatloaves with thinly sliced green onion and serve with small bowls of sweet chilli sauce.

hamburger with a twist

80g gorgonzola cheese, crumbled
¼ cup (60g) sour cream
400g beef mince
120g sausage mince
1 small brown onion (80g), chopped finely
1 tablespoon barbecue sauce
2 teaspoons worcestershire sauce
½ cup (75g) drained sun-dried tomatoes in oil, chopped finely
4 hamburger buns
50g baby rocket leaves
170g marinated artichoke hearts, drained, quartered

1 Blend or process half of the cheese with the sour cream until smooth. Stir in remaining cheese.
2 Using hand, combine minces, onion, sauces and tomato in medium bowl; shape mixture into four hamburger patties.
3 Cook patties in large lightly oiled heated frying pan until browned both sides and cooked through.
4 Meanwhile, halve buns; toast, cut-side up. Sandwich rocket, patties, gorgonzola cream and artichoke in toasted buns.

serves 4
per serving 29.2g total fat (14.1g saturated fat); 2579kJ (617 cal); 49.7g carbohydrate; 39g protein; 2.3g fibre

beef and bean tacos

1 clove garlic, crushed
80g beef mince
½ teaspoon chilli powder
¼ teaspoon ground cumin
300g can kidney beans, rinsed, drained
2 tablespoons tomato paste
½ cup (125ml) water
1 medium tomato (150g), chopped coarsely
4 taco shells
¼ small iceberg lettuce, shredded finely
salsa cruda
½ lebanese cucumber (65g), seeded, chopped finely
½ small red onion (40g), chopped finely
1 small tomato (90g), seeded, chopped finely
1 teaspoon mild chilli sauce

1 Preheat oven to moderate (180°C/160°C fan-forced).
2 Heat large lightly oiled non-stick frying pan; cook garlic
and mince, stirring, until mince is cooked through. Add chilli,
cumin, beans, paste, the water and tomato; cook, covered,
over low heat about 15 minutes or until mixture thickens slightly.
3 Meanwhile, place taco shells, upside-down, on oven tray;
heat, uncovered, 5 minutes.
4 Combine ingredients for salsa cruda in small bowl.
5 Just before serving, fill taco shells with mince mixture,
lettuce and salsa cruda.

serves 4
per serving 5.8g total fat (1.2g saturated fat); 757kJ (181 cal);
20.9g carbohydrate; 10.8g protein; 2.6g fibre

beef, tomato and pea pies

1 tablespoon vegetable oil
1 small brown onion (80g),
    chopped finely
300g beef mince
400g can chopped
    tomatoes
1 tablespoon tomato paste
2 tablespoons
    worcestershire sauce
½ cup (125ml) beef stock
½ cup (60g) frozen peas
3 sheets ready-rolled
    puff pastry
1 egg, beaten lightly

1 Heat oil in large saucepan; cook onion, stirring, until softened. Add mince; cook, stirring, until mince changes colour. Stir in undrained tomatoes, tomato paste, sauce and stock; bring to a boil. Reduce heat; simmer, uncovered, about 20 minutes or until sauce thickens. Stir in peas. Cool.
2 Preheat oven to moderately hot (200°C/180°C fan-forced). Oil 6-hole texas (¾-cup/180ml) muffin pan.
3 Cut two 13cm rounds from opposite corners of each pastry sheet; cut two 9cm rounds from remaining corners of each sheet. Place the six large rounds in muffin pan holes to cover bases and sides; trim any excess pastry. Lightly prick bases with fork; refrigerate 30 minutes. Cover the six small rounds with a damp cloth.
4 Cover pastry-lined muffin pan holes with baking paper; fill holes with uncooked rice or dried beans. Bake, uncovered, in oven, 10 minutes; remove paper and rice. Cool.
5 Spoon mince filling into holes; brush edges with a little egg. Top pies with small pastry rounds; gently press around edges to seal.
6 Brush pies with remaining egg; bake, uncovered, about 15 minutes or until browned lightly. Stand 5 minutes in pan before serving with mashed potatoes, if desired.

makes 6
per pie 26.1g total fat (3.3g saturated fat); 1873kJ (448 cal); 35.3g carbohydrate; 18.1g protein; 1.1g fibre

mexican beef pizza

1 tablespoon vegetable oil
500g beef mince
35g packet taco seasoning
1¾ cups (450ml) bottled thick 'n' chunky salsa
2 x 335g prepared pizza bases
2 cups (200g) pizza cheese
⅓ cup (80g) sour cream

1 Preheat oven to very hot (240°C/220°C fan-forced).
2 Heat oil in large frying pan; cook mince, stirring, until
cooked through. Add taco seasoning and 1½ cups (375ml)
of the salsa; bring to a boil.
3 Place pizza bases on pizza trays, spread with mince mixture;
sprinkle with cheese. Bake, uncovered, in oven about
20 minutes or until pizzas are browned and bases are crisp.
4 Serve pizzas topped with dollops of sour cream and
remaining salsa.

serves 4
per serving 40.2g total fat (18.5g saturated fat); 4167kJ (997
cal); 96.7g carbohydrate; 61.5g protein; 1.6g fibre
tip If you don't have a pizza tray, use an oven tray instead.

chile con carne

1 tablespoon olive oil
1 large brown onion (200g), chopped finely
1 clove garlic, crushed
3 fresh small red thai chillies, chopped finely
500g beef mince
2 x 400g cans chopped tomato
⅓ cup (90g) tomato paste
1½ teaspoons white sugar
1 cup (250ml) beef stock
420g can red kidney beans, rinsed, drained

1 Heat oil in large saucepan; cook onion, garlic and chilli, stirring, until onion softens. Add mince; cook, stirring, over medium heat until mince is cooked through.
2 Add undrained tomatoes, paste, sugar and stock, bring to boil; simmer, uncovered, stirring occasionally, about 25 minutes or until most of the liquid has evaporated.
3 Add beans; cook, covered, a further 10 minutes.

serves 4
per serving 13g total fat (3.9g saturated fat); 1467kJ (351 cal); 23.4g carbohydrate; 34.9g protein; 1.6g fibre
tips Beans must be rinsed well to remove all trace of the canning liquid. A can of refried beans may be used in place of the red kidney beans, if desired.
Serve chile con carne with corn chips or toasted tortilla wedges, or wrap in warm corn tortillas and top with sour cream and mashed avocado.

potato wedges with sloppy joe topping

4 medium potatoes (800g)
2 tablespoons olive oil
1 clove garlic, crushed
1 large brown onion (200g), chopped finely
1 small green capsicum (150g), chopped finely
1 trimmed celery stalk (100g), chopped finely
750g beef mince
2 tablespoons mild american mustard
2 tablespoons cider vinegar
1 cup (250ml) tomato sauce
½ cup (60g) coarsely grated cheddar cheese
2 green onions, sliced thinly

1 Preheat oven to hot (220°C/200°C fan-forced).
2 Cut each potato into eight wedges; place in large shallow baking dish, drizzle with half of the oil. Roast, uncovered, about 30 minutes or until wedges are tender.
3 Meanwhile, heat remaining oil in large frying pan; cook garlic, brown onion, capsicum and celery, stirring, until vegetables soften. Add mince; cook, stirring, until mince is changed in colour. Stir in mustard, vinegar and sauce; bring to a boil. Reduce heat; cook, stirring, until sloppy joe is cooked through and slightly thickened.
4 Serve wedges topped with sloppy joe mixture; sprinkle with cheese and green onion.

serves 4
per serving 25.8g total fat (9.2g saturated fat); 2537kJ (607 cal); 43.6g carbohydrate; 50.2g protein; 1g fibre
tip Thinly sliced green onion will go curly if placed in a small bowl of iced water.

lasagne bolognese

This is the way lasagne is traditionally made in Bologna, Italy – with chicken liver and milk in the sauce and long, slow cooking. You'll never go back to your old lasagne recipe again after you taste this version.

6 slices pancetta (90g), chopped finely
1 large white onion (200g), chopped finely
1 medium carrot (120g), chopped finely
2 trimmed celery stalks (200g), chopped finely
1kg beef mince
150g chicken livers, trimmed, chopped finely
2 cups (500ml) milk
60g butter
2 cups (500ml) beef stock
1 cup (250ml) dry red wine
410g can tomato puree
2 tablespoons tomato paste
¼ cup finely chopped fresh flat-leaf parsley
8 fresh lasagne sheets
2 cups (160g) finely grated parmesan cheese
white sauce
125g butter
¾ cup (110g) plain flour
1.25 litres (5 cups) hot milk

1 Cook pancetta in lightly oiled large heavy-based pan, stirring, until crisp. Add onion, carrot and celery; cook, stirring, until vegetables soften. Add mince and liver; cook, stirring, until mince changes colour. Stir in milk and butter; cook, stirring occasionally, until liquid reduces by about half. Add stock, wine, puree and paste; simmer, uncovered, 1½ hours. Remove from heat; stir in parsley.

2 Preheat oven to moderately hot (200°C/180°C fan forced). Grease deep 26cm x 35cm baking dish.

3 Make white sauce. Spread about ½ cup of the white sauce over base of dish. Layer two pasta sheets, one-quarter of the meat sauce, ¼ cup of the cheese and about 1 cup of the remaining white sauce in dish. Repeat layering process, starting with pasta sheets and ending with white sauce; you will have four layers in total. Top lasagne with remaining cheese.

4 Bake lasagne, uncovered, in oven about 40 minutes or until top is browned lightly. Stand 15 minutes before cutting.

white sauce Melt butter in medium saucepan, add flour; stir until mixture forms a smooth paste. Gradually stir in milk; bring to a boil, stirring, until sauce thickens.

serves 8
per serving 44.2g total fat (26.3g saturated fat); 3219kJ (770 cal); 36.9g carbohydrate; 52.6g protein; 0.5g fibre

cottage pie

1 tablespoon olive oil
2 cloves garlic, crushed
1 large brown onion (200g),
  chopped finely
2 medium carrots (240g),
  peeled, chopped finely
1kg beef mince
1 tablespoon
  worcestershire sauce
2 tablespoons tomato paste
2 x 400g cans
  chopped tomatoes
1 teaspoon dried
  mixed herbs
200g mushrooms,
  quartered
1 cup (120g) frozen peas
1kg sebago potatoes,
  peeled, chopped coarsely
¾ cup (180ml) hot milk
40g butter, softened
½ cup (50g) coarsely grated
  pizza cheese

1 Heat oil in large saucepan; cook garlic, onion and carrot, stirring, until onion softens. Add mince; cook, stirring, until mince changes colour.
2 Add sauce, paste, undrained tomatoes and herbs; bring to a boil. Reduce heat; simmer, uncovered, about 30 minutes or until mixture thickens slightly. Stir in mushrooms and peas.
3 Meanwhile, preheat oven to moderate (180°C/160°C fan-forced).
4 Boil, steam or microwave potato until tender; drain. Mash in large bowl with milk and butter.
5 Pour mince mixture into deep 3-litre (12-cup) ovenproof dish; top with mashed potato mixture; sprinkle with cheese. Bake, uncovered, in oven about 45 minutes or until pie is heated through and top is browned lightly.

serves 8
per serving 16.6g total fat (7.6g saturated fat); 1622kJ (388 cal); 24.3g carbohydrate; 35.1g protein; 1.3g fibre
tips You can make the cottage pie up to two days in advance; keep, covered, in the refrigerator.

beef burritos

4 x 25cm-round flour tortillas
1 cup (120g) grated cheddar cheese
1 teaspoon hot paprika
¾ cup (180g) sour cream
1 tablespoon chopped fresh coriander
bean and beef filling
1 tablespoon olive oil
1 medium brown onion (150g), chopped finely
1 clove garlic, crushed
500g beef mince
400g can chopped tomatoes
35g packet taco seasoning mix
½ cup (125ml) water
300g can kidney beans, rinsed, drained

1 Make bean and beef filling.
2 Preheat oven to moderately hot (200°C/180°C fan-forced).
3 Divide warm bean and beef filling among tortillas; roll to enclose filling, secure with toothpicks.
4 Place burritos on oiled oven tray; sprinkle with cheese then paprika. Bake about 10 minutes or until heated through.
5 Remove toothpicks; serve burritos topped with sour cream, coriander and, if desired, guacamole and salad.
bean and beef filling Heat oil in medium frying pan; add onion and garlic; cook, stirring, until onion is soft. Add mince, cook, stirring, until mince is cooked through. Stir in undrained tomatoes and remaining ingredients; simmer, uncovered, about 15 minutes or until mixture is thickened.

serves 4
per serving 44.2g total fat (22.8g saturated fat); 3031kJ (725 cal); 38.1g carbohydrate; 44.2g protein; 1.4g fibre
tips The burritos must be assembled just before serving. The bean and beef filling can be made a day ahead and stored, covered, in the refrigerator.

thai beef patties with noodle salad

250g dried rice stick noodles
800g beef mince
¼ cup (75g) red curry paste
2 tablespoons vegetable oil
250g cherry tomatoes, halved
1 lebanese cucumber (130g), halved, seeded, sliced thinly
4 green onions, chopped finely
1 medium red capsicum (200g), sliced thinly
1 cup (80g) bean sprouts
½ cup firmly packed fresh coriander leaves
½ cup (125ml) sweet chilli sauce
¼ cup (60ml) rice vinegar

1 Place noodles in large heatproof bowl, cover with boiling water, stand until noodles just soften; drain.
2 Using hand, combine mince and paste in medium bowl; shape mixture into 12 patties.
3 Heat oil in large frying pan; cook patties, in batches, until browned both sides and cooked through.
4 Meanwhile, combine tomato, cucumber, onion, capsicum, sprouts and coriander in large bowl. Add noodles and half of the combined sauce and vinegar; toss gently to combine.
5 Serve patties with noodle salad, drizzled with remaining sauce and vinegar mixture.

serves 4
per serving 28.2g total fat (6.9g saturated fat); 2282kJ (546 cal); 25.8g carbohydrate; 47g protein; 1.3g fibre
tip Patties can be shaped several hours ahead; store, covered, in refrigerator, until ready to cook.

sang choy bow

1 tablespoon sesame oil
1 medium brown onion (150g), chopped finely
2 cloves garlic, crushed
300g pork mince
300g veal mince
¼ cup (60ml) soy sauce
¼ cup (60ml) oyster sauce
1 medium red capsicum (150g), chopped finely
3 cups (240g) bean sprouts
3 green onions, chopped coarsely
1 tablespoon toasted sesame seeds
8 large iceberg lettuce leaves

1 Heat oil in wok; stir-fry brown onion and garlic until onion softens. Add both minces; stir-fry until cooked through. Add sauces and capsicum, reduce heat; simmer, uncovered, stirring occasionally, 3 minutes.
2 Just before serving, stir in sprouts, green onion and seeds. Divide lettuce leaves among serving plates; spoon sang choy bow into leaves.

serves 4
per serving 14g total fat (3.2g saturated fat); 1384kJ (331 cal); 11.4g carbohydrate; 39.3g protein; 1.3g fibre

glazed pork and veal apple meatloaf

2 teaspoons olive oil
1 small brown onion (80g), chopped finely
2 cloves garlic, sliced thinly
1 trimmed celery stalk (100g), chopped finely
1 medium green apple (150g), peeled, grated coarsely
250g pork mince
250g veal mince
1 cup (70g) stale breadcrumbs
1 tablespoon coarsely chopped fresh sage
1 egg
10 thin streaky bacon rashers
1 small green apple (130g), cored, sliced thinly, extra
2 tablespoons apple jelly (or redcurrant or quince jelly)

1 Heat oil in large frying pan, add onion, garlic and celery; cook, stirring, until onion is soft. Add apple; cook, stirring, until all the liquid has evaporated, cool.
2 Preheat oven to moderate (180°C/160°C fan forced).
3 Using hand, combine onion mixture with both minces, breadcrumbs, sage and egg in large bowl.
4 Transfer mince mixture to large sheet of plastic wrap; use wrap to roll mixture into 8cm x 24cm log, discard plastic. Wrap bacon around log, alternating extra apple slices with bacon.
5 Place meatloaf onto an oiled oven tray, brush all over with half of the warmed jelly. Roast, uncovered, in oven about 45 minutes or until meatloaf is cooked through and bacon is browned and crisp, brushing halfway through cooking with remaining jelly. Serve with mustard, if desired.

serves 4
per serving 18.4g total fat (5.9g saturated fat); 1898kJ (454 cal); 21.1g carbohydrate; 50.9g protein; 0.7g fibre

chicken kofta with red capsicum and walnut sauce

700g chicken mince
1 large brown onion (200g),
    chopped finely
1½ cups (110g) stale
    breadcrumbs
1 egg
¼ cup finely chopped
    fresh coriander
3 teaspoons ground cumin
2 teaspoons ground allspice
6 pitta pockets, halved
100g baby rocket leaves
red capsicum and
    walnut sauce
2 medium red
    capsicums (400g)
⅓ cup (35g) toasted walnuts
2 tablespoons stale
    breadcrumbs
2 tablespoons lemon juice
1 teaspoon sambal oelek
½ teaspoon ground cumin
2 tablespoons olive oil

1 Using hand, combine mince, onion, breadcrumbs, egg, coriander and spices in large bowl; shape ¼ cups of the mixture around each skewer to form slightly flattened sausage shapes. Place kofta on tray, cover; refrigerate 10 minutes.

2 Meanwhile, make red capsicum and walnut sauce.

3 Cook kofta on heated oiled grill plate (or grill or barbecue), uncovered, about 15 minutes or until cooked through. Serve kofta with warm pitta, rocket and red capsicum and walnut sauce.

red capsicum and walnut sauce Quarter capsicums; discard seeds and membranes. Cook on heated oiled grill plate (or grill or barbecue), skin-side down, uncovered, until skin blisters and blackens. Cover capsicum pieces with plastic wrap or paper for 5 minutes; peel away skin. Blend or process capsicum with remaining ingredients until smooth.

serves 4
per serving 28g total fat (4.7g saturated fat); 3486kJ (834 cal); 87.8g carbohydrate; 57g protein; 1.4g fibre
tip You need 12 bamboo skewers for this recipe. Soak them in cold water before use to prevent them from splintering and scorching.

onion and fennel risotto with chicken meatballs

1 litre (4 cups)
chicken stock
1 litre (4 cups) water
1 cup (250ml) dry white wine
1 tablespoon olive oil
20g butter
2 medium brown onions
(300g), sliced thinly
1 large fennel bulb (550g),
trimmed, sliced thinly
3 cups (600g) arborio rice
2 cloves garlic, crushed
1 cup (80g) coarsely grated
parmesan cheese
2 tablespoons finely
chopped fresh tarragon
chicken meatballs
500g chicken mince
1 egg
1 clove garlic, crushed
¾ cup (50g) stale
breadcrumbs
1 tablespoon finely
chopped fresh tarragon

1 Make chicken meatballs.
2 Combine stock, the water and wine in large saucepan; bring to a boil. Reduce heat; simmer, covered.
3 Heat oil and butter in large saucepan; cook onion and fennel, stirring, over low heat about 15 minutes or until vegetables soften.
4 Add rice and garlic to pan, stir to coat in butter mixture. Add 1 cup of the simmering stock mixture; cook, stirring, over low heat until liquid is absorbed. Continue adding stock mixture, in 1-cup batches, stirring, until liquid is absorbed after each addition. Total cooking time should be about 35 minutes or until rice is just tender. Gently stir chicken meatballs, cheese and half of the tarragon into risotto. Serve sprinkled with remaining tarragon.

chicken meatballs Combine ingredients in medium bowl. Roll level tablespoons of the mixture into balls. Cook meatballs in large lightly oiled frying pan, shaking pan occasionally, until browned all over and cooked through.

serves 6
per serving 19.3g total fat (7.8g saturated fat); 2918kJ (698 cal); 90.5g carbohydrate; 33.2g protein; 0.5g fibre

asian chicken burger with wasabi mayonnaise

1 lebanese cucumber
(130g), sliced thinly
¼ cup (70g) drained pickled
pink ginger
½ cup (125ml) rice vinegar
1 teaspoon salt
1 tablespoon white sugar
500g chicken mince
2cm piece fresh ginger
(10g), grated
1 tablespoon soy sauce
1 egg
1 cup (70g) stale
breadcrumbs
1 teaspoon sesame oil
2 green onions,
chopped finely
4 hamburger buns
50g mizuna
wasabi mayonnaise
¼ cup (75g) mayonnaise
2 teaspoons wasabi paste

1 Combine ingredients for wasabi mayonnaise in small bowl.

2 Combine cucumber in small bowl with pickled ginger, vinegar, salt and sugar. Cover; refrigerate 30 minutes.

3 Meanwhile, using hand, combine mince, fresh ginger, sauce, egg, breadcrumbs, oil and onion in large bowl; shape mixture into four patties.

4 Cook patties on heated oiled flat plate, uncovered, about 15 minutes or until cooked through.

5 Meanwhile, split buns in half horizontally; toast, cut-side up.

6 Spread wasabi mayonnaise on bun bases; sandwich mizuna, patties and drained cucumber mixture between bun halves.

serves 4
per serving 22g total fat (4.8g saturated fat); 2399kJ (574 cal); 57.7g carbohydrate; 35.2g protein; 1.3g fibre

chicken larb

2 tablespoons long-grain
white rice
1 tablespoon peanut oil
1 tablespoon finely
chopped fresh
lemon grass
2 fresh small red thai
chillies, chopped finely
2 cloves garlic, crushed
1 tablespoon finely
chopped fresh galangal
750g chicken mince
1 lebanese cucumber (130g),
seeded, sliced thinly
1 small red onion (100g),
sliced thinly
1¼ cups (100g)
bean sprouts
½ cup loosely packed
fresh thai basil leaves
1 cup loosely packed fresh
coriander leaves
4 large iceberg
lettuce leaves
dressing
⅓ cup (80ml) lime juice
2 tablespoons fish sauce
2 tablespoons kecap manis
2 tablespoons peanut oil
2 teaspoons grated
palm sugar

1 Heat dry wok; stir-fry rice until browned lightly. Blend or process rice (or crush using mortar and pestle) until it resembles fine breadcrumbs.
2 Heat oil in same wok; stir-fry lemon grass, chilli, garlic and galangal until fragrant. Remove from wok. Stir-fry mince, in batches, until cooked through.
3 Meanwhile, place ingredients for dressing in screw-top jar; shake well.
4 Return mince and lemon grass mixture to wok with about one-third of the dressing; stir-fry about 5 minutes or until mixture thickens slightly.
5 Place remaining dressing in large bowl with chicken mixture, cucumber, onion, sprouts and herbs; toss gently to combine. Place lettuce leaves on serving plates; divide larb salad among leaves, sprinkle with ground rice.

serves 4
per serving 29.1g total fat (7g saturated fat); 1969kJ (471 cal); 11.9g carbohydrate; 40g protein; 0.8g fibre

chicken gow gees

400g chicken mince
2 green onions,
　chopped finely
2 cloves garlic, crushed
2cm piece fresh ginger
　(10g), grated
¼ teaspoon five-spice
　powder
½ cup (50g) packaged
　breadcrumbs
1 tablespoon hoisin sauce
2 tablespoons coarsely
　chopped fresh coriander
1 egg
24 gow gee wrappers
sweet chilli dipping sauce
⅓ cup (80ml) sweet chilli
　sauce
¼ cup (60ml) red wine
　vinegar
¼ cup coarsely chopped
　fresh coriander

1 Using hand, combine mince, onion, garlic, ginger, five-spice, breadcrumbs, sauce, coriander and egg in large bowl. Roll level tablespoons of the mixture into balls; place balls on tray. Cover; refrigerate 30 minutes.
2 Meanwhile, place ingredients for sweet chilli dipping sauce in screw-top jar; shake well.
3 Brush one wrapper with water; place one chicken ball in centre of wrapper. Fold wrapper over to completely enclose chicken ball. Pleat edge of wrapper along join; repeat process with remaining wrappers and chicken balls.
4 Place gow gees, in single layer, about 1cm apart in baking-paper-lined steamer fitted over large saucepan of boiling water; steam, covered, about 8 minutes or until gow gees are cooked through.

serves 4
per serving 11.3g total fat (3.2g saturated fat); 1622kJ (388 cal); 42.5g carbohydrate; 32.2g protein; 1.1g fibre
tip Gow gee wrappers are found packaged in the refrigerated section of Asian grocery stores as well as in some supermarkets. Wonton or spring roll wrappers can be used instead.

minestrone with meatballs

400g pork mince
1 teaspoon sweet paprika
1 egg
1 medium brown onion (150g), chopped finely
¼ cup (70g) tomato paste
2 tablespoons olive oil
2 cloves garlic, crushed
2 medium carrots (240g), diced into 1cm pieces
1 trimmed celery stick (100g), diced into 1cm pieces
2 x 400g cans chopped tomatoes
2 cups (500ml) chicken stock
2 cups (500ml) water
2 large zucchini (300g), diced into 1cm pieces
400g can borlotti beans, rinsed, drained
½ cup (110g) risoni

1 Using hand, combine mince, paprika, egg, half of the onion and 1 tablespoon of the tomato paste in medium bowl. Roll level tablespoons of mixture into balls.
2 Heat oil in large saucepan; cook meatballs, in batches, until browned. Cook garlic and remaining onion in same pan, stirring, until onion softens. Add carrot and celery; cook, stirring, until vegetables are just tender.
3 Add remaining paste to pan; cook, stirring, 1 minute. Add undrained tomatoes, stock and the water; bring to a boil.
4 Add zucchini, beans, risoni and meatballs; return to a boil. Reduce heat; simmer, covered, about 15 minutes or until meatballs are cooked through.

serves 4
per serving 19.5g total fat (4.7g saturated fat); 2069kJ (495 cal); 44.5g carbohydrate; 34.9g protein; 1.4g fibre

pork burgers with caramelised pears

500g pork mince
2 cloves garlic, crushed
3 green onions,
    chopped finely
1 fresh small red thai
    chilli, chopped finely
1 egg
2 tablespoons
    barbecue sauce
½ cup (35g) stale
    breadcrumbs
4 small pears (720g),
    sliced thinly
1 medium red onion (170g),
    sliced thinly
¼ cup (60ml) balsamic
    vinegar
1 tablespoon brown sugar
1 long french bread
    stick (350g)
2 tablespoons dijonnaise
50g mizuna

1 Using hand, combine mince, garlic, green onion, chilli, egg, sauce and breadcrumbs in medium bowl; shape mixture into four patties. Cook patties on heated oiled flat plate, uncovered, until cooked through.

2 Meanwhile, cook pear and red onion on heated oiled flat plate, uncovered, until onion softens. Sprinkle combined vinegar and sugar over pear and red onion; cook, turning, about 10 minutes or until mixture caramelises.

3 Cut bread into quarters; split quarters in half horizontally. Spread dijonnaise on cut sides; sandwich mizuna, patties and caramelised pear and red onion between bread pieces.

serves 4
per serving 14.2g total fat (4.2g saturated fat); 2521kJ (603 cal); 81.4g carbohydrate; 37.5g protein; 1.6g fibre

tips We used corella pears, small pears with pale flesh and a mild flavour, for this recipe.
Dijonnaise is a commercial blend of mayonnaise and dijon mustard; it is available in most supermarkets.

spaghetti and meatballs

500g pork mince
2 tablespoons coarsely chopped fresh flat-leaf parsley
1 clove garlic, crushed
1 egg
1 cup (70g) stale breadcrumbs
1 tablespoon tomato paste
2 tablespoons olive oil
400g can chopped tomatoes
600ml bottled tomato pasta sauce
375g spaghetti
⅓ cup (25g) finely grated romano cheese

1 Using hand, combine mince, parsley, garlic, egg, breadcrumbs and paste in large bowl; roll tablespoons of mixture into balls. Heat oil in large saucepan; cook meatballs, in batches, until browned all over.
2 Place undrained tomatoes and tomato sauce in same pan; bring to a boil. Return meatballs to pan, reduce heat; simmer, uncovered, about 10 minutes or until meatballs are cooked through.
3 Meanwhile, cook pasta in large saucepan of boiling water, uncovered, until just tender; drain.
4 Divide pasta among serving bowls; top with meatballs, sprinkle with cheese.

serves 4
per serving 24.2g total fat (6.5g saturated fat); 3206kJ (767 cal); 89.2g carbohydrate; 46.6g protein; 1.6g fibre
tips The meatballs can be made and fried a day ahead; store, covered, in the refrigerator until the sauce is made. Reheat as per step 2.

lamb patties with beetroot and tzatziki

500g lamb mince
1 small brown onion (80g), chopped finely
1 medium carrot (120g), grated coarsely
1 egg
2 tablespoons finely chopped fresh flat-leaf parsley
1 teaspoon finely grated lemon rind
½ teaspoon dried oregano
2 cloves garlic, crushed
½ cup (140g) yogurt
1 lebanese cucumber (130g), seeded, chopped finely
1 tablespoon finely chopped fresh mint
1 loaf turkish bread (430g)
1 cup (60g) coarsely shredded cos lettuce
225g can sliced beetroot, drained
1 medium lemon (140g), cut into wedges

1 Using hand, combine mince, onion, carrot, egg, parsley, rind, oregano and half of the garlic in medium bowl; shape lamb mixture into four patties. Cook patties on heated oiled grill plate (or grill or barbecue) until cooked as desired.
2 Meanwhile, combine yogurt, cucumber, mint and remaining garlic in small bowl. Cut bread into four pieces; split each piece in half horizontally. Toast bread cut-side up.
3 Sandwich lettuce, patties, beetroot and yogurt mixture between bread pieces. Serve with lemon wedges.

serves 4
per serving 17.3g total fat (6.7g saturated fat); 2324kJ (556 cal); 57.3g carbohydrate; 40.7g protein; 1.5g fibre

lamb pide

2 small brown onions (160g), chopped finely
2 cloves garlic, crushed
250g lamb mince
1 tablespoon tomato paste
¼ teaspoon hot paprika
1 teaspoon ground cumin
2 small turkish breads
¼ cup (25g) finely grated low-fat mozzarella cheese
2 tablespoons chopped fresh mint

1 Preheat oven to hot (220°C/200°C fan forced).
2 Cook onion and garlic in lightly oiled medium saucepan, stirring, until onion softens. Add mince, paste, paprika and cumin; cook, stirring, until mince is cooked through.
3 Split breads; place bases on oven tray. Spread with mince mixture; sprinkle with cheese and mint. Replace tops; bake pide, uncovered, in oven about 10 minutes or until bread is crisp. Cut each pide in half to serve.

serves 4
per serving 7.9g total fat (3.4g saturated fat); 928kJ (222 cal); 18.6g carbohydrate; 19g protein; 1.4g fibre
tip Turkish bread is also known as pide.

moussaka

2 large eggplants (1kg),
  sliced thinly
1 tablespoon coarse
  cooking salt
¼ cup (60ml) olive oil
1 large brown onion (200g),
  chopped finely
2 cloves garlic, crushed
1kg lamb mince
400g can chopped
  tomatoes
½ cup (125ml) dry white
  wine
1 teaspoon ground
  cinnamon
¼ cup (20g) finely grated
  parmesan cheese
white sauce
80g butter
⅓ cup (50g) plain flour
2 cups (500ml) milk

1 Place eggplant in colander, sprinkle all over with salt; stand 30 minutes. Rinse under cold water; drain. Pat dry with absorbent paper.

2 Heat oil in large frying pan; cook eggplant, in batches, until browned both sides; drain on absorbent paper.

3 Cook onion and garlic in same pan, stirring, until onion softens. Add mince; cook, stirring, until mince changes colour. Stir in undrained tomatoes, wine and cinnamon; bring to a boil. Reduce heat; simmer, uncovered, about 30 minutes or until liquid has evaporated.

4 Meanwhile, preheat oven to moderate (180°C/160°C fan-forced). Oil shallow 2-litre (8-cup) rectangular baking dish.

5 Make white sauce.

6 Place a third of the eggplant, overlapping slices slightly, in dish; spread half of the meat sauce over eggplant. Repeat layering with another third of the eggplant, remaining meat sauce and remaining eggplant. Spread white sauce over top layer then sprinkle with cheese.

7 Cook, uncovered, in oven about 40 minutes or until top browns lightly. Cover moussaka; stand 10 minutes before serving.

white sauce Melt butter in medium saucepan. Add flour; cook, stirring, until mixture thickens and bubbles. Gradually add milk; stir until mixture boils and thickens.

serves 6
per serving 39.8g total fat (18g saturated fat); 2567kJ (614 cal); 18.7g carbohydrate; 42.9g protein; 1g fibre

glossary

arborio rice small round-grain rice; well suited to absorb a large amount of liquid, especially good in risottos.

artichoke hearts tender centre of the globe artichoke. Artichoke hearts can be purchased in brine, canned, or in glass jars, or fresh.

basil we used sweet basil, unless otherwise specified. *Thai basil* is different from sweet basil in both look and taste. Having smaller leaves, purplish stems, and a slight licorice or aniseed taste.

breadcrumbs, packaged purchased, fine-textured, crunchy, white breadcrumbs.

butter use salted or unsalted (sweet) butter; 125g is equal to one stick of butter.

cabbage
  chinese also known as napa or peking cabbage, wong bok or petsai. Elongated in shape with pale green, crinkly leaves.
  savoy has large, heavy head with crinkled dark-green outer leaves; fairly mild tasting.

capers sold either dried and salted or pickled in a vinegar brine; tiny, young baby capers are also available.

char sui sauce a chinese barbecue sauce made from sugar, water, salt, fermented soy bean paste, honey, soy sauce, malt syrup and spices. Found at most supermarkets.

cheese
  fetta a crumbly textured goat or sheep-milk cheese with a sharp, salty taste.
  gorgonzola creamy blue cheese with mild, sweet taste.

mozzarella soft spun-curd cheese; has a low melting point and a wonderfully elastic texture when heated.

parmesan also known as parmigiano; a hard, grainy cow-milk cheese.

pizza cheese a commercial blend of varying proportions of processed grated mozzarella, cheddar and parmesan.

romano originally pecorino romano. A hard, sheep or cow-milk cheese. Straw-coloured and grainy in texture. Parmesan can be substituted.

chilli use rubber gloves when seeding and chopping chillies as they can burn your skin. Removing membranes and seeds lessens the heat level.

hot chilli sauce we used a hot Chinese variety made from birdseye chillies, salt and vinegar.

ciabatta means 'slipper' in Italian, which is the traditional shape of this popular white bread with a crisp crust.

coriander also known as pak chee, cilantro or chinese parsley; bright-green leafy herb with a pungent flavour. Both the stems and roots of coriander can be used.

cornflour thickening agent, also known as cornstarch.

cream, thickened whipping cream containing a thickener.

fish sauce also known as nam pla or nuoc nam; made from pulverised salted fermented fish (most often anchovies). Has pungent smell and strong taste; use according to your taste.

five-spice powder also known as chinese five-spice powder. A fragrant mixture of ground cinnamon, cloves, star anise, sichuan pepper and fennel seeds.

flour, plain an all-purpose flour, made from wheat.

galangal also known as ka, a rhizome with a hot ginger-citrusy flavour; used similarly to ginger and garlic. Fresh ginger can be substituted for fresh galangal, but the flavour will not be the same.

ginger, fresh also known as green or root ginger; the thick gnarled root of a tropical plant.

gow gee wrappers wonton wrappers, spring roll or egg pastry sheets can be substituted, if required.

hoisin sauce a thick, sweet and spicy chinese paste made from salted fermented soy beans, onions and garlic.

kecap manis also known as ketjap manis. A thick soy sauce with added sugar and spices.

lemon grass a tall, clumping, lemon-smelling and tasting, sharp-edged grass; the white lower part of the stem is used, finely chopped, in cooking.

mizuna Japanese in origin; frizzy green salad leaf having a delicate mustard flavour.

mushrooms, button small, cultivated white mushrooms with a mild flavour.

mustard, wholegrain also known as seeded. A coarse-grain mustard made from crushed mustard seeds and dijon-style French mustard.

noodles

dried rice stick also known as sen lek, ho fun or kway teow. Come in different widths. Should be soaked in hot water until soft.

fresh egg also known as ba mee or yellow noodles. Range in size from very fine strands to wide, thick spaghetti-like pieces as thick as a shoelace.

oil

olive made from ripened olives. *Extra virgin* and *virgin* are the first and second press, respectively, and are considered the best, while *extra light* or *light* are diluted and refer to taste, not fat levels.

vegetable sourced from plants rather than animal fats.

onion

green also known as scallion or, incorrectly, shallot; an immature onion picked before the bulb has formed, having a long, bright-green edible stalk.

red also known as spanish, red spanish or bermuda onion; a sweet-flavoured, large, purple-red onion.

oyster sauce made from oysters and their brine, cooked with salt and soy sauce and thickened with starches.

pancetta cured pork belly; bacon can be substituted.

parsley, flat-leaf also known as continental parsley and italian parsley.

pide also known as turkish bread. Comes in long (about 45cm) flat loaves as well as individual rounds; made from wheat flour.

pine nuts also known as pignoli; not, in fact, a nut, but a small, cream-coloured kernel from pine cones.

prosciutto salt-cured, air-dried (unsmoked) pressed ham.

puff pastry, ready rolled packaged sheets of frozen pastry, which are available from supermarkets.

red curry paste a combination of dried red chillies, onions, garlic, oil, lemon rind, shrimp paste, ground cumin, paprika, ground turmeric and ground black pepper.

risoni small rice-shaped pasta.

rocket also known as arugula, rugula and rucola; a green, peppery-tasting leaf.

sage pungent herb with narrow, grey-green leaves; slightly bitter with a slightly musty mint aroma. Refrigerate fresh sage wrapped in a paper towel and sealed in a plastic bag for up to four days. Dried sage comes whole, crumbled or ground. It should be stored in a cool, dark place for no more than three months.

sambal oelek (also ulek or olek); a salty paste made from ground chillies and vinegar.

soy sauce made from fermented soy beans.

stock 1 cup (250ml) stock is the equivalent of 1 cup (250ml) water plus 1 stock cube (or 1 teaspoon stock powder).

sugar

brown a very soft, fine granulated sugar retaining molasses for its characteristic colour and flavour.

palm sugar also called jaggery; made from the sap of the sugar palm tree. Light brown to black in colour and usually sold in rock-hard cakes; substitute brown sugar if it is unavailable.

taco seasoning mix a packaged seasoning meant to duplicate the Mexican sauce made from oregano, cumin, chillies and other spices.

tomato pasta sauce a prepared tomato-based sauce; comes in varying degrees of thickness and spicing.

tortilla thin, round unleavened bread originating in Mexico; can be purchased frozen, fresh or vacuum-packed.

vinegar

balsamic made from white Trebbiano grapes specially processed to give the exquisite pungent flavour.

cider made from fermented apples.

rice a colourless vinegar made from fermented rice and flavoured with sugar and salt. Also known as seasoned rice vinegar. Sherry can be substituted, if preferred.

wasabi an asian horseradish used to make a pungent, green-coloured sauce; sold in powdered or paste form.

water chestnuts small brown tubers with a crisp, white, nutty-tasting flesh. Best fresh, however, canned are more easily obtained and can be kept about a month, once opened, under refrigeration.

worcestershire sauce a thin, dark-brown spicy sauce.

conversion chart

MEASURES

One Australian metric measuring cup holds approximately 250ml, one Australian metric tablespoon holds 20ml, one Australian metric teaspoon holds 5ml.

The difference between one country's measuring cups and another's is within a two- or three-teaspoon variance, and will not affect your cooking results. North America, New Zealand and the United Kingdom use a 15ml tablespoon.

All cup and spoon measurements are level. The most accurate way of measuring dry ingredients is to weigh them. When measuring liquids, use a clear glass or plastic jug with the metric markings.

We use large eggs with an average weight of 60g.

DRY MEASURES

METRIC	IMPERIAL
15g	½oz
30g	1oz
60g	2oz
90g	3oz
125g	4oz (¼lb)
155g	5oz
185g	6oz
220g	7oz
250g	8oz (½lb)
280g	9oz
315g	10oz
345g	11oz
375g	12oz (¾lb)
410g	13oz
440g	14oz
470g	15oz
500g	16oz (1lb)
750g	24oz (1½lb)
1kg	32oz (2lb)

LIQUID MEASURES

METRIC	IMPER
30ml	1 fluid
60ml	2 fluid
100ml	3 fluid
125ml	4 fluid
150ml	5 fluid oz (¼ pint/1
190ml	6 fluid
250ml	8 fluid
300ml	10 fluid oz (½ p
500ml	16 fluid
600ml	20 fluid oz (1 p
1000ml (1 litre)	1¾ pi

LENGTH MEASURES

METRIC	IMPER
3mm	1
6mm	1
1cm	1
2cm	3
2.5cm	
5cm	
6cm	2½
8cm	
10cm	
13cm	
15cm	
18cm	
20cm	
23cm	
25cm	1
28cm	1
30cm	12in (

OVEN TEMPERATURES

These oven temperatures are only a guide for conventional ovens.
For fan-forced ovens, check the manufacturer's manual.

	°C (CELSIUS)	°F (FAHRENHEIT)	GAS MARK
Very slow	120	250	½
Slow	150	275 – 300	1 – 2
Moderately slow	160	325	3
Moderate	180	350 – 375	4 – 5
Moderately hot	200	400	6
Hot	220	425 – 450	7 – 8
Very hot	240	475	9

index

Are you missing some of the world's favourite cookbooks?

The Australian Women's Weekly cookbooks are available from bookshops, cookshops, supermarkets and other stores all over the world. You can also buy direct from the publisher, using the order form below.

MINI SERIES £3.50 190x138MM 64 PAGES

TITLE	QTY	TITLE	QTY	TITLE	QTY
4 Fast Ingredients		Grills & Barbecues		Roast	
4 Kids 2 Cook		Healthy Everyday Food 4 Kids		Salads	
15-minute Feasts		Ice-creams & Sorbets		Simple Slices	
50 Fast Chicken Fillets		Indian Cooking		Simply Seafood	
50 Fast Desserts		Italian Favourites		Soup plus	
Barbecue Chicken		Indonesian Favourites		Spanish Favourites	
Biscuits, Brownies & Bisottti		Jams & Jellies		Stir-fries	
Bites		Japanese Favourites		Stir-fry Favourites	
Bowl Food		Kebabs & Skewers		Summer Salads	
Burgers, Rösti & Fritters		Kids Party Food		Tagines & Couscous	
Cafe Cakes		Lebanese Cooking		Tapas, Antipasto & Mezze	
Cafe Food		Low-Fat Delicious		Tarts	
Casseroles & Curries		Low Fat Fast		Tex-Mex	
Char-grills & Barbecues		Malaysian Favourites		Thai Favourites	
Cheesecakes, Pavlova & Trifles		Mince Favourites		The Fast Egg	
Chinese Favourites		Microwave		The Young Chef	
Chocolate Cakes		Muffins		Vegetarian	
Crumbles & Bakes		Noodles & Stir-fries		Vegie Main Meals	
Cupcakes & Cookies		Old-Fashioned Desserts		Vietnamese Favourites	
Dips & Dippers		Outdoor Eating		Wok	
Dried Fruit & Nuts		Packed Lunch			
Drinks		Party Food			
Easy Pies & Pastries		Pickles and Chutneys			
Fast Fillets		Pasta			
Fishcakes & Crispybakes		Potatoes			
Gluten-free Cooking		Quick Desserts		TOTAL COST £	

Photocopy and complete coupon below

Name _____

Address _____

_____ Postcode _____

Country _____ Phone (business hours) _____

Email*(optional) _____
* By including your email address, you consent to receipt of any email regarding this magazine, and other emails which inform you of ACP's other publications, products, services and events, and to promote third party goods and services you may interested in.

I enclose my cheque/money order for £ _____ or please charge £ _____ to my:
☐ Access ☐ Mastercard ☐ Visa ☐ Diners Club

Card number | | | | | | | | | | | | | | | |

3 digit security code *(found on reverse of card)* _____

Cardholder's signature _____ Expiry date ___ /___

To order: Mail or fax – photocopy or complete the order form above, and send your credit card details or cheque payable to: Australian Consolidated Press (UK), 10 Scirocco Close, Moulton Park Office Village Northampton NN3 6AP, phone (+44) (01) 604 642200, fax (+44) (01) 604 642300, e-mail books@acpuk.com or order online at www.acpuk.com
Non-UK residents: We accept the credit cards listed on the coupon, or cheques, drafts or International Money Orders payable in sterling and drawn on a UK bank. Credit card charges are at the exchange rate current at the time of payment. All pricing current at time of going to press and subject to change/availability.
Postage and packing UK: Add £1.00 per order plus 75p per book.
Postage and packing overseas: Add £2.00 per order plus £1.50 per book. **Offer ends 31.12.2008**